George Cadenhead, Aberdeen Philosophical Society

Sketch of the Territorial History of the Burgh of Aberdeen

George Cadenhead, Aberdeen Philosophical Society

Sketch of the Territorial History of the Burgh of Aberdeen

ISBN/EAN: 9783337379803

Printed in Europe, USA, Canada, Australia, Japan

Cover: Foto ©Thomas Meinert / pixelio.de

More available books at **www.hansebooks.com**

SKETCH

OF

THE TERRITORIAL HISTORY

OF THE

BURGH OF ABERDEEN.

ENLARGED FROM A PAPER READ BEFORE THE
ABERDEEN PHILOSOPHICAL SOCIETY
ON 11TH JANUARY, 1876.

BY

GEORGE CADENHEAD,

PROCURATOR FISCAL.

ABERDEEN : LEWIS SMITH.
1878.

NOTE.

THE following Paper, in a shorter form, was read at a meeting of the Aberdeen Philosophical Society on 11th January, 1876, and was appointed, after revision and enlargement, to be printed amongst the Transactions of that Society ; which has accordingly been done.

ABERDEEN, *July*, 1878.

SKETCH OF THE TERRITORIAL HISTORY OF THE BURGH OF ABERDEEN.

THE design of this Essay is to trace and describe the ancient land-marks and "meaths" and marches of the territories pertaining to Aberdeen as a Royal Burgh; to explain the purposes which the various territorial divisions answered in their day, and to shew how they originated. It is not proposed to extend the enquiry to the social, political, or mercantile affairs of our Burghal predecessors, nor to take notice of those lands which have come into the possession of the Burgh in trust for charitable or educational purposes. Very much that is interesting has been, and more remains to be, written on the ancient interests and manners and customs of the people of our Burgh, but there is a distinct and peculiar interest in the enquiry here proposed which will be abundantly sufficient for the narrow space within which it will necessarily be treated.

These ancient territorial divisions are sufficiently well known to enable us to see clearly, even if we had nothing else to guide us, that there had been a system and a plan in their origination; and recent historical and archæological researches have shewn us, that over many parts of the earth, where our Aryan races have had their habitations, similar or kindred systems and plans are traceable as to the manner in which they portioned out and used their lands. The noticeable characteristic of these old systems, was the holding by communities of definite tracts of land divided into three sections, viz., 1st., the village or town, in which were the dwelling-houses; 2nd., the arable section, which was devoted to cultivation under certain regulations; and 3rd., the common lands, which were de-voted to pasturage and the production of fuel. This is altogether such a system as we should expect to find adopted by communities belonging to a race accustomed to establish its colonies in new and hostile lands; the dwelling-places being grouped closely together for neighbourhood and defence; the arable lands being as near the

1

defensible town as possible ; and the common pasture land, from which the cattle could be driven in when danger approached, being outside and around the arable land.   But if these early races had been possessed with our modern ideas of private property in land, we should have found the arable section at least divided and appropriated by individuals, each doing with his own section as he pleased. Such, however, was not the case.   The idea of absolute private right in land, except, perhaps, within the town section, was entirely unknown.   Such an idea was excluded, and for long ages rendered impossible by the prevalence of the opposite idea, that the use of the land was a common and joint life-rent right of the community. In accordance with this idea, it appears that, while each family in the town had right to a section of the arable land, all were bound to adhere to a certain routine of cultivation and rotation of crops ; that when one part of the arable land was for a time deserted in order to lie fallow, all were obliged to take and cultivate sections in the portion next chosen for cultivation, and there is sufficient reason to believe that periodically, in order to preserve equality of occupation, there were redistributions of the arable sections amongst the families. *

Such is the system which seems to have been inveterate in the habits of the Teutonic races, and as these races are believed to have established a footing in very early times along the north-eastern coasts of Scotland, it will be interesting, but not surprising, to find traces of them in the ancient territorial divisions of the Burgh of Aberdeen.

An enquiry into the origin of the name *Aberdeen*, and into the question as to whether our Royal Burgh or the Old Town is the older, may not be strictly relevant to the design of this essay, but both questions are sufficiently interesting to excuse their introduction and brief discussion.   There is a common but really irrational tendency on the part of citizens of the Royal Burgh to claim for it the credit of being older than the sister city, and of having been the first to bear the name.   But all known facts seem to be against the claim.   No doubt there have been towns or settlements at the mouths of both rivers at periods remote beyond our ken, and into the seniority of which it would be uninteresting to enquire, even

---

* "Village Communities in the East and West"—by Henry Sumner, Maine. London, 1871.

if we had the means ; but some one of these had, in times more nearly within our reach—viz., after the advent of the Celtic race— come to bear the name of Aberdeen, and that name had ultimately attached itself to a town at the mouth of each river, and we wish to know where the name was originally located.

First then, we cannot without good reason set aside the fact that our earliest information—viz., a Charter by King David in 1134— speaks of the two towns as then bearing respectively the names of Aberdeen and Old Aberdeen, which simply means that at that date our Royal Burgh was regarded as the younger of the two ; and historically we have no farther information on the subject.

Secondly, an examination of the name philologically leads to the same conclusion. We have no trace of such a name as *Aberdee* having ever existed ; and if it had existed unknown to us, no explanation could be given of how the letter *n* should have been added to the end of it. The River Dee is believed to have derived its name from an ancient Celtic root meaning *God*, and in all probability it had in ancient times, like the Welsh Dee, been regarded for some reason as a sacred stream ; but that root gives no suggestion of the name ever having terminated with or having a tendency to assume an *n* for its termination, or of ever having admitted the letter *o* into its composition.

On the other hand, the River Don is supposed to have derived its name from an ancient Celtic word meaning *deep*, wherein the *o* is a prominent sound and the final *n* is a necessity. The earliest mention of Aberdeen also, viz., in a charter of King David's, copied in the Book of Deer, gives the name as *Abberdeon*. The Latin language, as used by lawyers, churchmen, and historians, has tenaciously adhered to *Aberdonia* as the name of both towns, and in later times the name is often given broadly as *Abirdon*.

The fact seems to be that originally the name had been neither *Aberdon* nor *Aberdeen*, but an intermediate sound like *Aberdoon*, and the well-known tendency of the local tongue to change such words as boots, shoon, moon, poor, &c., into *beets*, *sheen*, *meen*, *peer*, &c., had inevitably changed the sound into what we now find it. The community of name thus supposed is not altogether unimportant, since it suggests the idea that, although somewhat scattered, the component parts of both towns had originally gone to form one political community ; and this idea is countenanced by some facts to be afterwards adverted to.

As we know from the Book of Deer that the Christian Church was planted in Buchan as early as the seventh century, we have no reason to doubt that it had been planted in Aberdeen very soon after, if not as soon, or sooner; and the position of the earliest chapels between Dee and Don mouth may serve to indicate to us the places where the population was greatest, and where the aboriginal villages or towns were situated.   Beginning at the north side of the district, we learn, on the authority of Mr. Orem, who was Town-Clerk of Old Aberdeen from 1691 to about 1726,* that before 1134, when the Bishop's See was transferred to its present site from Mortlach, Old Aberdeen was a village of four ploughs, that is, with common arable lands extending to about four hundred acres, and had a " little kirk" where the Cathedral now stands, called the Kirk of Kirktown, dedicated to Saint Machar.   On the same authority we learn that a little south of the Old-Town College stood the parish church of Old Aberdeen, called Saint Mary of the Snow, and a little way south of that a chapel dedicated to Saint Peter, both obliterated and almost forgotten in 1661.

Passing then to Dee mouth we find that of old there had been a chapel at Futtie, which Mr. Gordon, Parson of Rothiemay (1661),† says was " a paroshen by itselff," and from the fact of the shore opposite to it being the harbour for boats, nearest to the sea, we may say that it is not unlikely that the community of Futtie was as ancient as any in the neighbourhood.   Farther west we come to Saint Catherine's Hill, in the close neighbourhood of which there had been, how anciently we cannot tell, a Royal Palace and a chapel. This locality, as will be afterwards shewn, has the appearance of having been also a very ancient centre of population, and, probably, the nucleus of what ultimately became the town and Royal Burgh of Aberdeen.   Lastly, the site of Saint Nicholas Parish Church had, probably, been that of one of the primitive churches or chapels. The same Mr. Gordon says, that the Old Kirk there " began to be builded by the citizens about the yeir 1060."   By that time it is likely that the population had spread pretty thickly towards the

---

* "A description of the Chanonry Cathedral and King's College of Old Aberdeen, in the years 1724 and 1725 "—by William Orem, Town-Clerk of Old Aberdeen.   J. Chalmers & Co., Aberdeen, 1791.

† "A Description of both towns of Aberdeen "—by James Gordon, Parson of Rothiemay.   Printed for the Spalding Club, 1842.

district lying between the flourmill and the loch where Tannery Street formerly was, and Saint Nicholas Church had been intended to accommodate the general population of the town, for which the original small chapels had become insufficient.

By about the year 1000 there seems reason to conclude that the town of Aberdeen, soon to be distinguished as the Burgh of Aberdeen, had taken something like the shape it had when the same Mr. Gordon, in 1661, made his interesting and instructive sketch or map, which was reproduced and published by the Spalding Club in 1842.

The derivation of the term Burgh, by which so many Scottish towns came to be distinguished, is very curious and of great antiquity. The Scottish Burghs seem to have been formed and named after the English Borows, and these seem to have been formed and named after the pattern of similar institutions in various countries of Europe. Defence, and not trade, seems to have been the motive for the formation of the Burghs. The name, however, was derived not from the sort of ground on which the towns stood, or from the defensive works which surrounded them, but from a class of men to whom their defence was entrusted, and it is probable that Trade had been the original motive of the association of that class of men. In the old Leges Burgorum and other ancient laws of Scotland, as translated in the fifteenth century, we are struck with the frequent recurrence of the word " borch," meaning in all cases a cautioner or surety, and in our ancient burghal institutions we find that in the practice of trade there was a law that every seller of any commodity should " streik a borch " (find security by a cautioner) that he had a good title to sell ; and every man engaging in a lawsuit or appealing against a judgment was obliged in like manner " to streik a borch." Words of the same sound and meaning also occur in all or most of the Teutonic languages. In the German language particularly the word *Bursch* or *Bursche,* plural *Burschen,* seems to be of extreme antiquity, and indicates an association of men, involving the idea of mutual aid or suretyship, without reference to locality. This term (borch) we had, no doubt, brought with us from the Continent of Europe, perhaps from a more remote locality, but it is traceable in Britain for nearly twelve hundred years, with the appearance of still greater antiquity. We read in Sir Thomas Murray of Glendook's treatise, " De Verborum Significatione," as follows :—" Frie Borgh.—In the auld Britton Laws Bopher vel Bores is that quhilk we call Borrows, borgh or cautioner—and Alured King of England divided England in satrapias, centurias et decurias : and ordained that decuria suld comprehend ten persons, and centuria suld contain 100 persons, quhairof ilk one was cautioner and sourtie for others ; in sik sort that the haill number and ilk ane of them was answerable for the fault and dede of anie ane of them, and swa was called free-borgh, free pledge or cautioner. Vide Antiquas leges Brittonum." This carries back the institution to the end of the ninth century, and to the laws of the Saxons of Wessex. But on referring to those ancient Britton Laws we find that the institution was well established at least a century and a half earlier ; for in the Laws of Hlothhaere and Eadric, Kings of Kent, 673—686, we find that the institution of suretyship and also towns were distinguished by the same name. In the translation of those laws, published in 1840 by the Commissioners of Public Records, a King's or Royal Burgh is rendered *Burh*, and a cautioner is rendered *Borh*, as if they were distinct words, and this has been done apparently to prevent readers from mistaking one for the other ; but on referring to the Saxon text both are found to be the same, the former being "*burig*" and the latter "*burigan.*"

Gradually the name "burg" or "borow" began to be applied to many of the English towns, formerly known as "tuns" or "wics," but it seems to have been several centuries later that Scottish towns came to be called by that name, earlier in the south, later in the north ; and we shall see that long after the inhabitants of these towns were distinguished as *burgesses* or *burghers*, the towns which they possessed were not invariably called burghs, but were simply called towns (villae).

In Scotland the Burghal institution seems to have been created before it had become usual to issue formal written charters. The first general charter in which both burghs and burgesses are mentioned, was granted by King David, on the 28th day of March, in the 34th year of his reign [1363], and it deals entirely with trade privileges, saying nothing of defence. This charter seems to have been preserved somewhere till the 24th May, 1605, when the Lords of Council "in respect that the said chartour is grantit in favours of the haill burgesses of Scotland, and speciallie concernis thame and evrie ane of thame, and that the said chartour is of sic great antiquitie quhairby in process of time the samin will nocht faill to perische and becum unlegibill, be the quhilk occasion the saidis frie burgessis of this realme haveand speciall interes thairto will be greatumlie hurte and damnefeit and prejudgeit in thair liberteis and privileges grantit to thame thairby," ordained the same to be transumed and "insert in the buikis of Counsaill in authentick forme ad perpetuam rei memoriam." The charter is as follows :—" David dei gracia Rex Scotorum Omnibus probis hominibus tocius terre sue clericis et laicis Salutem. Sciatis nos cum consilio (&c.) concessisse dilectis nostris burgensibus Scotie facultatem emendi et vendendi liberam ubique infra libertatem suorum burgorum prohibendo ne aliquis eorum infra limites alterius emat vel vendat nisi licentiatus.. Prohibemus etiam ne Episcopus aut Prior vel persona eclesiastica. Comes Baro vel persona secularis emat lanam pelles coria aut alia mercimonia sub quocunque colore cuius— cumque fuerit status neque vendat nisi solummodo a mercatoribus burgorum infra quorum resident quibus precipimus quod huiusmodi mercimonia presentent apud forum et crucem burgorum ut mercatores emant et ipsis effectualiter proferunt sine fraude et ibidem soluant custumam. Regis Prohibemus etiam ne aliqui extraniei mercatores cum nauibus et mercandisis venientes vendant aliquod genus mercimoniorum nisi mercatoribus nostrorum burgorum sub pena Regie defensionis nostre. Quasquidem concessiones libertates constitutiones pro perpetuo duraturas tenore presentis carte nostre confirmamus. In cuiis rei testimonium presenti carte nostre confirmationis sigillum nostrum precepimus apponi (apud Perth xxviii. die mensis Martii anno regui nostri trigesimo quarto). Testibus venerabillibus in Christo patribus Willelmo Episcopo Sanctiandree. Patricio Episcopo Brechinensi Cancellaris Roberto Senescallo Scotie nepote nostro. Willelmo comite de Dowglas Roberto de Erskyne Camerario nostro."

Of the original act or ceremony by which a town was converted or erected into a Royal Burgh or into a Burgh of minor status, we have no record. There is no specimen of any formal written deed of any Burgh until after King David's days ; and yet we can see that prior to this charter there must have been an extensive family of Burghs already erected. We learn, however, from the Leges Burgorum, that in order to entitle a Burgher to the privileges of his order he was bound to acquire and build upon and " defend " a certain measure of land within a Burgh, and it also appears that the leading characteristic of a Royal Burgh was that it should be the seat of a royal castle garrisoned by royal troops, under the command of a Constable of the king, and which the burghers and neighbouring barons had to aid in garrisoning and defending, by contributing men for that purpose. Barons and ecclesiastics, also, who possessed or were superiors of Burghs north of the Grampians were obliged to build and maintain castles within their bounds.* As to the particular manner of declaring that a town had taken its place in the family of Burghs, one may suppose that when the castle was built and occupied there had been some open-air assembly of the inhabitants held, and proclamation of the fact made to the sound of trumpet, &c., and so the fact would be accomplished and the preservation of its memory committed to the grasp of living testimony and oral tradition, more tenacious in these days than in ours.

In some such way as this, and at a time not now known, the town of Aberdeen, at the mouth of the Dee, had been converted into a Burgh of the King, and its inhabitants, who had the necessary qualification, invested with the dignity and privileges of "burgenses domini regis," or "kingis borowmen."

Our Burgh was never officially or correctly called *New* Aberdeen. Several writers, Mr. Gordon, Parson of Rothiemay, included, have called it so, but this has evidently been done to avoid a misapprehension as to which of the towns he was at the time writing of, and in the earliest records our Burgh appears simply as Aberdeen. As to the title of our Burgh to be called a City also, discussions have been raised, and many people believe that Old Aberdeen has a preferable right to that title as having been the seat of a bishop. But this has nothing to do with the question. The title of City seems to have been one of courtesy, indicating merely magnitude and importance, and we have an authority, as nearly infallible on this point as could be wished, where Pope Clement, in a bull, confirming the incorporation of the University of Old Aberdeen, refers to that institution thus, "Dilecti Filii, Rector Principalis et alii magistri Universitatis Studii generalis Ville veteris prope civitatem Aberdonem nobis humiliter applicari fecerunt."

Probably the first charter in which Aberdeen is mentioned was one granted by King David to the Clerics of Deir, and copied by them into their book, the exact date of which seems to be unascertained. It is given, "apud Abberdeon," and refers to certain privileges of these Clerics, written in their book.—"on which they pleaded at Banff and swore at Aberdeen (sicut in libro eorum scribtum est et diriationauerunt apud banb etjuraurunt apud Abberdeon)," from

---

* Stat. James I. Sec. 82, 1426.

which we may infer that Aberdeen was then for the time the head-quarters of the King's Court, where he had heard and given judgment on such questions. As there is no mention of the Bishop of Aberdeen amongst the numerous witnesses to this charter, it seems not unlikely that it had been granted prior to 1134, when a Bishop was translated from Mortlach to Old Aberdeen.

The next mention of Aberdeen is found in a charter granted also by King David I., at Forfar, in the 13th year of his reign (1134). This charter is not, I believe, extant; but Mr. Orem, in his *" Description of the Chanonry, Cathedral, and King's College of Old Aberdeen, in the years 1724 and 1725,"* gives it at length. The mention of our Burgh in this charter is brief, but interesting. The King thereby grants " to God and the Blessed Mary, St. Machar, and Nectanus, Bishop of Aberdeen (Episcopo Aberdonensi), the haill village of Old Aberdon, &c. ——; the tithe of the ships called Snows (canium navium) which come to Aberdon; the tithe of victual there; my own tithe of the revenues of Aberdeen; the tithe of the Thanage revenues and escheats belonging to me within the Sheriffdom of Aberdeen and Banff, &c." So here, in 1134, we have mention made familiarly of Aberdeen and Old Aberdon, even as at the present day; and we learn that even then great ships resorted to our harbour. As to these ships called Snows, the " skeely skippers" of the port would no doubt have been more amused than surprised if they had been told that the King's lawyers knew so little about ships as to translate a snow into *navis cana*, or *candida*, a white ship; the truth being that *snau* or *schnau*, the vernacular name of these vessels, meant a snout or beak. They were ships probably of the largest size used for merchandise, with a fore and mainmast, and having an exaggerated beak in front of the forecastle to enable them to carry a jib-boom, and therefore more headsail. In later days these vessels had a rudimentary mizenmast on the top of the tall castle on the poop; and it is no doubt these snaws which we see represented in Mr. Gordon's map, and in that wonderful picture of the town and harbour of Aberdeen which is placed above the fireplace in our town-hall.

The earliest charter granted specially to Aberdeen was by King William the Lyon, in or about the year 1179. It confirms certain mercantile rights to " my burgesses of Aberdoen," but makes no mention of lands, territories, or boundaries. It also makes mention of burgesses elsewhere in the north of Scotland; but does not apply the name Burgh to Aberdeen or to any other place. The whole drift of the charter is to assure to the King's burgesses of Aberdeen, and all the burgesses of Moray, and all the King's burgesses dwelling on the north side of the Grampians, their ancient right of holding what is latinised as " ansum ;" and which is believed to have referred to a mercantile League or Bond, which existed amongst our merchants, and probably identical with that which afterwards took the form of the Hanseatic League amongst the merchants of the Continent of Europe.

A second charter by King William the Lyon about the year 1196 deals entirely with personal privileges to the Burgesses " de Aberdon," and does not name either burgh or territories.

Our third charter is by King Alexander II., of date 1226. By it the king grants to his " burgh and burgesses of 'Aberden' the same rights and privileges which his predecessors gave to the burgh and burgesses of Perth ;" and it enumerates those privileges referring exclusively to trade. But in fact there is no appearance of Perth having received any earlier privileges than Aberdeen, or any earlier charters ; only it was becoming the fashion for the king, when confirming an old right, to refer to it as having been originally conferred by his predecessors ; and this practice long persevered in led ultimately to the general belief that all rights had flowed originally from the king. This clause contains a remarkable reservation, which I have not found commented on elsewhere. After repeatedly mentioning the county and the Burgh of Aberdeen, as distinguished from each other ; thus, for example—" A stranger merchant within the County of Aberden, beyond the Burgh of Aberden," it concludes thus—" All these liberties and usages, however, I grant, and by this my charter confirm to them, without prejudice to the liberties and free usages which before this grant were given to other burghs and burgesses within the Bailliwic of Aberdeen (infra balliam de Aberden)." To expiscate and explain the meaning of this quotation might require much study and research, and what little I can say about it, will be more conveniently brought forward after I have gone over the territories of the Burgh in detail.

It is to be observed that at this time (1226), the process of feudalising the land tenures in Scotland was not only not completed, but had not made much progress; and we have as yet no indication of that process having been applied to the Royal Burghs of Scotland. The land did not, as yet, in theory belong to the king, and those who possessed it were not " vassals" of the king, or of any subjects representing the king in the characters of baillies, aldermen, maors, barons, thanes, or earls. An owner of land at that time held it by what is now called allodial tenure ; he owed allegiance and service to the State, as one of the community, and paid to the king, or the king's representative, a certain tax, in proportion to the extent of land he owned. As yet, accordingly, we have no formal gift by the king of the Burgh to the community ; because as yet the Burgh did not in theory belong to the king, but to the community itself. The feudal theory, however, was progressing, and holders of land were becoming accustomed to feel that in order to secure the recognition of their old rights by the crown, it was desirable to have them acknowledged by written deeds.

Accordingly, in pursuance of this feeling there was obtained from King Alexander III., of date about (1277), a charter, the gist of which is, " Know that our burgesses of Aberden have justly assumed possession of (suscepisse) their lands, their men, and their universal possessions, and all their goods, moveable and immoveable (neither the word nor the full idea of *heritable* being yet developed), under our assured peace and protection." The word " suscepisse " has apparently been chosen as a compromise between expressions which on the one hand should have too broadly asserted the king's right to give, and on the other hand should have too plainly allowed the right of the grantees to have and to hold without such gift.

I cite the next instrument merely to show that in its day the title of burgess seemed to be of more importance to burgesses than the title of burgh was to the town they dwelt in ; and in corroboration of my remark that the burgess class seemed to have importance more in their character of an association of men than as the inhabitants of a burgh. It is a commission by the " Custodes Regni" in 1287, to certain men to hear and determine a dispute which had arisen between the burgesses and community of Aberdeen on the one part, and the burgesses and community of Montrose on the other part— " Super nundinis villarum de Abirden et de Munros (concerning the markets of the towns of Abirden and Munros)." It may be that the " Custodes Regni" did not share the willingness which the preceding kings had shown to foster and exalt the Burghs as an element of the State, and that while they could not ignore the burgesses amongst whom, expressly in their character of burgesses, this dispute had arisen, they were willing to ignore the Burghs themselves, and that hence they designated them by the humbler name of towns.

The next instrument shows more care and discrimination in this matter. It is a petition by the burgesses of Banff, of date 1289, to the " Custodes Regni," to settle a difference which had arisen as to the interpretation of the charter of King Alexander II., before referred to ; and here the petitioners design themselves, " Prepositi ac ceteri burgenses commune de Banff," while Aberdeen is carefully designed as a Burgh, the fact being, that although Banff now claims to have been then a Royal Burgh, it was not formally acknowledged as such till 1372. In this petition the burgesses of Banff, although probably believing that they were king's burgesses, had abstained from claiming that dignity, in case a question raised on that point should have hindered or prevented the hearing of their petition.

We now come to the year 1313 when the pressure upon occupiers and claimants of land to take out charters had become strong. To the west of the Burgh of Aberdeen there lay a large tract of waste land, called the Forest of Stocket, which the community of Aberdeen had possessed for pasturage and fuel, and over which their Magistrates had no doubt exercised jurisdiction as governors ; but it was also a King's Forest, and used by the King as a hunting ground. Here there was doubtless a field for three competing claims which would become more troublesome the longer it remained unchartered, viz., the Aberdeen people claiming the use of it as their waste ; other neighbours encroaching and founding similar claims ; and the King, whose claim would gather strength the more the other two disputed over it. For the King's lawyers would say that whatever did not belong to other people belonged to the King; and, therefore, other disputants in weakening each other's claims, strengthened that of the King. The claim of Aberdeen, however, had been recognised as good, and a charter had been demanded ; but the difficulty was what the charter should convey. There had, at the same time, been an arrangement in contemplation for changing the allodial tenure of the Burgh of Aberdeen into a feudal tenure, and it had not been determined what place, if any, the Forest of Stocket should hold in the new feudal grant. As a temporary arrangement, King Robert I., in 1313, granted a charter or commission to the burgesses and community of the Burgh of Abirden to have the care and custody of the whole Forest of Stocket "to be held and had by the said Burgh, Burgesses, and Community of the same, and their heirs and successors," the green trees and right of hunting only being reserved. In contemplation of obtaining a better right this had no doubt been regarded as satisfactory, and it had the effect of excluding all others from the Forest in the meantime ; but this of itself would have been a dangerous title to stand upon, for it might have been open to the Crown afterwards to plead, if it had taken the trouble to plead on the subject, that this was only a commission during the King's pleasure, and in the meantime the old consuetudinary rights of the Burgh would have been receding into the dim and uncertain region of the things that had been.

In 1320, however, King Robert I. granted a regular feudal charter, in the form then in use, to the burgesses and community of the Burgh of Aberdeen, of the Burgh of Aberdeen and the Forest of Stocket in perpetuity " in fee and heritage and in free burgage," with mills, waters, fishings, petty customs, tolls, courts, weights, measures, and with all other liberties, conveniences, easements, consuetudes, and their just pertinents belonging, or which in future should belong, to the sett (assedacionem) of the said Burgh and Forest by law and use and wont, paying therefor yearly to the King or his heirs the sum of two hundred and thirty pounds six shillings and eight pence.

And thus the feudalising process, as between the King and the Burgh, was completed, and hereafter the Burgh, instead of paying a sum corresponding to each rood and acre of land occupied by its citizens, paid a fixed sum annually to the King, who was acknowledged to be the proprietor of the land, while the Burgh acknowledged that it held the land on a perpetual lease.

Subsequently, by various charters and Acts of Parliament of the times of James VI. and Charles I., the former charters were confirmed, and the rights and jurisdictions elaborately set forth, and three other pieces of land were also incorporated with the Burgh. The first of these was Rubislaw. This had probably been a town-land lying close to the Burgh on the west, and had either not belonged to the Burgh originally, or had been detached from it, and given to some other overlord. In 1359 a part of it belonged to a Burgess of Aberdeen, and a certain " John de Inchecur," is designated "dominus de Rubislaw." By 1379 it had been acquired, probably bought, by the Burgh, and in that year King Robert II. granted it to the Burgh, of Aberdeen to be held in fee and heritage in free Burgage. The second was the land of Cruives, which John Bannerman of Alsike conveyed to the Burgh, for a price no doubt ; but these old deeds say nothing about prices. In conveying this land it is, in 1459, described as " anciently spoken of as le smythyhalch (the smithy haugh) in modern days, called le Croes." This also was subsequently incorporated with the Burgh. The third was the land or territory of Futty, a name since corrupted into Footdee—whereas the original name seems to have been brought from Norway by Scandinavian emigrants. There seems to be great probability that Futty had originally been a Townland distinct from the Burgh, which had subsequently absorbed it. A considerable marsh had once separated it from the Burgh, and, as I have remarked before, it had certainly been, very early, the seat of a fishing population. In 1413 mention is made of a citizen bearing the name of " Laurentius de Futty," which founds a prima facie presumption that he or his ancestors had stood in the position of proprietors or overlords of that land ; and in many old deeds it is referred to as " the territory of Futty," " the town of Futty," and " Futtieland." It was never very formally granted to the Burgh ; but in one of the elaborate Crown charters before mentioned, it is included as " the green medow near the City, called Futtie."   ⸜

One other territory remains to be mentioned, because it was entirely surrounded by the Burgh and its territories, but was never included amongst them. This is the land of Gilcomston, comprehending about 340 Scotch acres, close to the Burgh on the north-west. This land had belonged to the Earl of Marr, and was feudalised in his possession. It passed from him to " John de Ross," and thereafter to the family of Menzies, who sold it to the Burgh in 1680. But it never was incorporated with the Burgh, nor was it subject to its taxes or jurisdiction. It is described as a Five Pound land of old extent, and corresponds roughly with three ploughlands with some addition of waste, or with four ploughlands with something lost by the accidents of time. It seems probable that this land was the seat of an ancient community, where Jack's Brae and Loanhead now are ; and we find that on one occasion the Town Council met and transacted business at Gilcomston, because the plague was in the Burgh.

The charter granted by King Charles I. in 1638, is the most elaborate of all that have been obtained by the Burgh. It doubtless contains nothing beyond what the Burgh had before, but in conformity with the legal usages of the time, it contains full catalogues of rights and privileges, which, according to the older practice, were taken for granted, and were proveable by use and wont and ancient possession. It may be well to rehearse, as shortly as possible, what this charter of Charles I. confirms. They are—the Burgh of Aberdeen, with precinct, walls, ditches, gates, &c.—lands within the territory and liberty of the Burgh—the forest of Stocket, with its pertinents—the lands of Rubislaw—the lands of Cruiffeis— the waters of Dee and Don, with the salmon fishings therein, as then possessed and occupied, particularly the Raik, Stells, Medchingle, Pot and Fuirds, on both sides of the Dee, from the bar at the river mouth, to the bridgewater at the Bridge of Dee—the King's Cavill fishing in Don, as well above as below the bridge, and the fishing of Cruives, from Don mouth to Cruive burn—the salmon and white fishing in the sea, between Dee and Don mouths, and on both sides of these river mouths—the insches and scheils, " infra et super," the waters of Dee and Don—the right of having ferry-boats, one or more, on both sides, where the said fishings are—the Upper and Lower Justice Mills—a mill on the Bucksburne, and another on the Denburne—the windmill at Gallowgate-head—two sea mills at the shore—the right to build more mills—the castlehill, the green medow and suburb called Futtie, with the chapel thereof, with all boats and white fishings pertaining thereto, and, with the bulwark port and shore (littore) of Aberdene, and milldams and passages thereof—the liberty and privilege of " loading and lousing " ships boats and others whatsoever, in Dee and Don, on either banks thereof —the right of collecting petty customs, anchorages, and " schoir silver," and other duties, as the Burgh of Edinburgh collects the same at the port and harbour of Leith, or at any other port and harbour in Scotland, a tax to support the bullwark—the Bell and Petty Customs, and tolls and other customs, used and wont—Tron and other weights—all lands, &c., which formerly belonged to whatsoever abbeys, priories, preceptories, chaplainries, prebendaries, alterages, and other benefices—the Common Loch—the hills called Womanhill, Playfield, Saint Catherineshill, Heidinghill, and Gallow- hill—the fields and plains called the Links between the watermouth of Dee and the watermouth of Don "—besides a number of jurisdic- tions and rights which need not be enumerated in a description pro- fessing to refer to territories only.

In addition to this, the Magistrates of the Burgh received a series of commissions from the Grand Admiral of Scotland to act as his deputies, and by virtue of these commissions they exercised an extensive and important maritime jurisdiction. They also regulated and limited the number of the fishing boats to be used in the port ; they divided the sea into beats, and every year on a certain day, at a certain hour, the boats were started and made a race for the respective beats, and the boat which first reached and claimed any beat had the sole use of it during the year.

The right of collecting shore-dues in the harbour at the mouth of the Dee is now represented by the powers in that behalf of the Harbour Commissioners. The same right was also exercised in Donmouth so long as it was worth the expense of collection.

I must again repeat that these various grants of King Charles's charter, the ecclesiastical properties excepted, are not to be regarded as rights conferred by King Charles or any other king, but only as an articulate rehearsal of the ancient rights of the Burgh as they were possessed, and established by custom when and before King Robert I. granted his first formal charter of the Burgh.

I now proceed to notice shortly the various component parts of the Burgh, with its Freedom and the Forest of Stocket.

As already mentioned, a Royal Castle was the special kenmark of a Royal Burgh. There might apparently be a body of King's Burgesses in a town ; but without a Royal Castle the Burgh was not a Royal one. Aberdeen had its Royal Castle on the Castle Hill, that is where the Barracks now stand. It is very likely that it may have been built by King David I., but this is uncertain. Its main purpose had been to afford a tenable stronghold against English assailants arriving by sea ; but it was found not only to be untenable, but to afford a temptation to these chronic enemies to take and occupy it. However, it turned out to be as untenable by the English as by the Scotch, and it was ultimately thrown down and abandoned ; and thereby hangs a tale. We have not full particulars of the following episode, but it seems likely that it had been represented to the Crown lawyers of the day that since Aberdeen no longer possessed a Royal Castle, it was no longer a Royal Burgh ; and if so, why should it possess any of the valuable pertinents of a Royal Burgh, that could be taken from it. This *ex parte* argument had seemed good to the Crown lawyers, and as the party urging it was no less a personage than Sir Andrew Wood, our celebrated admiral, it seems that without more ado the Castle Hill and the Forest of Stocket were conferred by a Royal Charter on Sir Andrew, and about the year 1494 he proceeded to claim possession of his gift. Had this attempt been successful we need be at no loss to guess what would have followed. Sir Andrew would next have got a charter of the whole burgh, that is of all the rights in it belonging to the king. He would have become the superior of the burgh, and Aberdeen would have subsided into a Burgh of Barony, ceasing to be a part of the fabric of the State, and thereafter its interests would not have been regarded or dealt with on public grounds, but solely with reference to the interests of the superior. But this was not to be, for on the 28th January, 1494, the citizens came to the following resolution :—" The saide day, the aldirmane, balyeis, consale, and communite, warnit be the hand bell throw the haile toune, gathreyit (this was a genuine head court) and circual inquerit be Philip Dumbrek, officiar, grauntit and oppinly schew that tha wald ayfaldly (unanimously) defende thair landis and heretage of the Stokat, baith with thair personis and gudis, at all thair possibilite, quhilkis is purchest be Androw Wod as thai are informit." In the following May several resolutions were adopted to the same effect, and as Sir Andrew's claim was brought forward before the Lords of Council, Commissioners were appointed " to pass til Edinburghe " and oppose the claim. It is evident that the Aberdonians were prepared to fight the battle legally in the first place, and if the decision had been adverse to them, we can imagine the gusto with which, in the imperative statutory language of the period,* they would have declared the doome to be " FALS, STINKAND, AND ROTTEN," by way of constitutional appeal against it ; but that they would have girded on their swords and resisted the execution of the decree by force, there cannot be a doubt. Such extreme measures turned out to be unnecessary, however, for Sir Andrew Wood did not produce his charter to the Lords of Council, who, on 19th June, 1494, having had the charter of the Burgh and Forest by " Robert the Broise, of moust nobill mynde," laid before them, decreed " that for ocht that thai have yit sene, the said Alderman, Baillies, and Communitie sall broik and joise the said Burgh of Abirdene, with the pertinence as thai brokit of before."

Starting from the Castle Hill as a central point, we look for the next characteristic mark of an ancient Royal Burgh—viz., the four quarters into which it was divided. This division was universal in the Royal Burghs. Four bailies and four quarters ; each bailie

---

* Stat. 9th James I., Sec. 116, 1429.

having a quarter under his special superintendence. It does not seem probable that the outer boundaries of the quarters were at any time fixed and unalterable; neither was the number of burgesses limited. It seems that the bounds of the quarters might be extended so as to accommodate each burgess with at least the statutory portion of land which he was bound to hold, to build upon, and to defend, and for which he had to pay yearly a tax or scat to the amount of five pence. "Ilke burges sall geyff to the King for his borowage at he deffendis (quod defendit), far ilke rud of land V d. be yhere." (Leg. Burg. I.)

It may not be tedious to hear the explanation given by the said Sir Thomas Murray of this primitive measure of land:—"Rood. It is of veritie that three beare cornes without tailes, set togidder in length makis ane inch; of the quhilk cornes, ane suld be taken off the mid rig, ane off the side of the rig, and ane off the furrow. Three fute and ane inch makes an elne; sex elnes lang makis ane fall; quhilk is the common lineall measure and mette. And sex elnes lang and sex elnes broad maks ane squair and superficiall fall of measured land. And it is to be understand ane rod, ane raip, ane lineall fall of measure, are all ane and signifies one thing, for ilk ane of them conteinis sex elnes in length, albeit ane rod is ane staffe or gade of tymmer quhairwith land is measured. Ane raip is made of towe, sik as hempe, or uther stuffe, and sa meikle land as in measuring falles under the rod or raip in length is called ane fall of measure ane lineal or fall. Likeas the superficial fall is the measure both of the length and the bredth. Item, ten falls in length and foure in bredth makes ane ruid; foure ruid makes ane aiker. And swa ane discreit and true man may measure ilk aiker of land, lang or schort, with rod or raip be the measure of the fall, swa that he keips just count and guid remembrance that the ends of the rod or raip be richtly and even laide, without fraude or guyle."

The 49th Article of the Leges Burgorum is as follows:—

"Of hym that yharnis to be mayd Kyngis burges, na man may be the Kyngis burges bvt gif he do service to the Kyng of als mekyl as fallys til ane rude of lande at the leste." The 7th Article of Enquiry, at the Chamberlain airs, was—"Gif the bailies have given saising of any land beyond what is defended;" and the 27th Article of the Leges Burgorum is—"Wha sum evir be made new burges of a waste land, and he hafe na lande wythin the burgh herberyit (inhabited), in the first yere he sall haf kyrset (respite or delay), and efter the fyrst yere he sall haf herberyit lande and byggyd." From all which provisions we see that a burgess must have at least one rood within the burgh " herberyit and byggyd "—that he may have more land than one rood ; but that the bailies had to see that sasine was not given of more land than was " defended;" by which it was probably meant that land which was not hitherto built upon and inhabited within the burgh required, when given off, to be fenced and walled in contiguously to the other defended lands, so as to form a compact and integral part of the defensible town.

This seems to provide for the case of a thriving and increasing Burgh, with new burgesses being constantly added to its former number ; so that the bailies might assign new sites out of the suburban land to be built and inhabited, or at least fenced, taking due care to preserve the Burgh in a compact and defensible form.

The four quarters would therefore increase in size, as new enclosures were made on their outer boundaries. Whether this was originally contemplated in the institution of town lands we cannot tell. Where agriculture was the chief, and trade only a secondary interest of the community, it is probable that any increase of the village mark at the expense of the agricultural land would have been regarded with jealousy and disfavour. But where trade was the chief occupation of the community, the reverse would be the case ; and where the community consisted of a body of trading burgesses, who alone probably had a right to the occupation and use of any part of the town lands, it is evident that public opinion, and therefore custom, would be in favour of the village mark being indefinitely increased. This probably had been the case of all the royal burghs ; and therefore if we attempt to define the ancient limits of the quarters of Aberdeen, our description will only be true for the particular date to which the description applies. We have of date 1764, ——— a description of the Four Quarters of Aberdeen—minute and distinct as to the divisions of one quarter from another, although somewhat indefinite as to their outer boundaries ; but as it would appear that Aberdeen had attained a certain pretty distinct size and shape at the time that the feudalizing process was about completed, and as it seems to have continued of that size and shape for a good many hundred years, and as the sasine records and old maps enable us to describe the burgh so shaped and defined pretty exactly, I shall confine my description of the Quarters to the area so defined—leaving it to be understood that the Quarters had no doubt once been of smaller extent, and that ultimately they expanded to a greater size.

No amount of narrative description, even to one familiar with Aberdeen, could convey so clear an idea of the appearance of the burgh in the year 1661, as a glance at Mr. Gordon's map made in that year ; and for the purpose of securing such clear idea to the reader a portion of that map is lithographed to illustrate this Essay. Such as Aberdeen then was in size and figure, there is some reason to believe it had been for more than three hundred years before—and such, with little change, it continued for a hundred years later, and even till the commencement of the present century. About the year 1850, the writer conversed with an old gardener, of the name of Alexander Smith, then about 80 years old, residing near the new Bridge of Don, who described the Aberdeen of his youth as being altogether like that described in Mr. Gordon's map ; and, as I have said, the sasine and other records indicate that in the fourteenth century the "herberyt byggyd and defended" Burgh of Aberdeen had occupied pretty exactly the area there described. Notwithstanding the changes of the last seventy years, any one acquainted with Aberdeen will easily recognise what was comprehended in the old Burgh. The outline ran from the east end of the "Peer," where one of the ships, called "snows," is riding, between the Heading and Castle Hill, along by the line of East and West North Street, by the foot of the east slope of the Gallow Hill to the Windmill, across the Gallowgate, then along the foot of the west slope of Gallowhill to the foot of the Vennel (St. Paul Street), across to the west side of Sillerton (Gordon's Hospital Grounds), along by Schoolhill and Woolmanhill to the Denburn, down the Denburn to the Harbour, and along the north side of the Harbour to the spot where it began. The Quarters had their common centre about the junction of Broadgate, Castlegate, and Shiprow, and were named respectively the Futty, the Green, the Crooked, and the Even Quarters. The two former names indicate their places. The Green Quarter comprehended Saint Catherine's Hill, and the space immediately west of it to the Bow Brig. The Futty Quarter comprehended the space immediately east of Saint Catherine's Hill to the Castle Hill. The Even Quarter comprehended the half of the large space north of the Green Quarter on the west of Guestrow and Gallowgate. The Crooked Quarter comprehended the remaining space north of Castlegate, and east of Guestrow and Gallowgate. It will at once be noticed that the two last-mentioned Quarters comprehended a much larger area than the two first mentioned, which, assuming that the Quarters had originally been of equal areas, favours the theory that the town had, in its early stages of growth increased and spread away towards the north more than in other directions.

The Gates or Ports next claim our attention. Our Burgh had six of these ; but we learn from Article 29 of "Fragmenta Quaedam veterum Legum et Consuetudinum Scotiae undique Collecta," that four was the number which an ancient Royal Burgh ought to have, and that probably this number was a notable kenmark of a Royal Burgh, even as the four Quarters were. This fragment commences thus, "Burges or merchandis or pipouderous (Dusty feet or Pedlars), when thai pas utouth the iiij yettis." Two of our six gates had therefore probably been added at some unknown time. The Trinity Port was across the mouth of the Shiprow, a little west of the head of Shorebrae. The Futty Port was at the south-east corner of the Castlegate, at the head of Hangman's Brae. The Justice Port was at the north-east corner of Castle Street. The Gallowgate Port was in Gallowgate, near the windmill. The Upperkirkgate Port was near the foot of Upperkirkgate, about the mouth of Burn Court probably. The Netherkirkgate Port was at the foot of Netherkirkgate, a little west of the south end of Flourmill Lane. These Ports or Gates seem to have been solid heavy walls, pierced by an archway, like Temple Bar in London, the Bar of Southampton, and other old English Burghs. Ours were removed in or about the year 1768, as being useless and obstructive to the streets.

The "walls" and "fosses or diches" of Aberdeen have given rise to disputes ; the question at issue being, whether they ever existed or not. But there is, in truth, no room for question on the subject. The fact that the Burgh was provided with gates or ports is *prima facie* evidence that the other parts of its outline were closed up in some defensible manner, and the passages already quoted from the old Laws indicate that the building upon and defending of the roods occupied by the burgesses, meant that the building should be so managed as to conduce to the defence of each particular piece of ground. Then if we look again at Mr. Gordon's map, we find exactly what, under these circumstances, one should expect, that the roods or building areas were contiguous and so grouped that the defences of each were part of the defences of the whole. We know,

indeed, that Aberdeen was not, in the ordinary sense of the words, a
walled town, that is, it had not a continuous line of external walls
distinct from the buildings of the town itself ; but we learn from
sure testimony that the defences naturally afforded by the house and
garden walls were supplemented where needful by walls and ditches
specially constructed for defence.   In 1452, a head court of the inhabitants determined that " the toune sal be stryngthnit and fortifiit
with walles, and strynthes in all gudeli haste," and a committee was
appointed to determine what should be done, and to have it done.
In 1480, March 17, denunciation is made of those who oppose the
making of the " fossis about the toune ;" and in 1481 another committee is appointed to " devise, see, and provide for the making of
the fossis, and performing of the walling of this toune, for the
strinthing of the sammyn."   All this, however, scarcely proves that
the walls and fosses were actually made ; but one may trust to the
accuracy of Mr. Gordon's knowledge when, writing about one
hundred and eighty years later, he says—" The unevne ground that
the toune is situated upon makes it quyt incapable of walls, or diches,
or bastions, according to the moderne invention of fortificatione ; yit
during the time of the civill warre, twyce, bot in vayne, it was
attempted to be fortified, or rather intrenshed about.   At both
tymes, scarce were the works perfytted when they were throwne
doune againe by the command of such as for the tyme seized the
toune."   We have no record of the lines of those defensive works
which seem to have consisted more of ditches than of walls ; but I
am told that within the present century there was a wall or part of
a wall running along the east side of Flourmill Lane, which was
believed to have been part of these defences.   In looking at Mr.
Gordon's map, it will be seen that this had been a comparatively
open place, and that the ground immediately to the west, between
that wall and the Saint Nicholas Kirk, was almost clear of buildings.
The same map also shews, at the present line of Virginia Street,
markings immediately north of the Shorelands ditch, which look like
representations of an earthwork and a wall or stockade on the top
of it.   Probably a military engineer, looking at that map, could
indicate pretty exactly where the works had been.

In considering the defences of the town, also, we must not over-
look that even now we can in many places perceive how the land of
each burgess was made in itself an independent and pretty secure
stronghold.   Take for example Stewart's Place in Guestrow, and

we see that the house next the street was in itself a fortification on that side—that a low gate gave entrance to an inner courtyard around which several houses were comfortably built, and that the back walls of these houses, and strong high walls enclosing the ground behind, completely closed in the whole space, and made it capable of easy defence against any assault by enemies not provided with military engines for battering down mason work. I hope that some one having the necessary skill will take the trouble to delineate and make accessible to the public descriptions of a number of these interesting nooks and corners before they are finally improved away and obliterated.

Before leaving the ancient Burgh, as built and defended, I would again draw attention to Mr. Gordon's map, and particularly to the representation of Saint Catherine's Hill there given. It will be observed that it is almost circular, and is entirely surrounded with buildings; that it is contiguous to the Quay head, and that two of the ports are on its margins. The present levels of the ground are so different from what they were at the beginning of this century, and even thirty years ago, that we have some difficulty in recognising the propriety of its being called a hill. But behind the houses on the east side of Adelphi, the crown of the hill, or part of it, is still visible; and the steep slope of the Shiprow, the Netherkirkgate, and Carnegie's Brae, still remain. The making out of Union Street had obliterated a great part of the north side of the hill; and the laying out and erection of Market Street on a line of tall arches on the west side almost completed its obliteration. But allowing for these changes, we can realize the fact that this hill had once been a well-defined and commanding eminence. Its closeness to the Quay head, along with its natural capabilities for defence, would strongly indicate it as having been the centre point of the original town which grew into the Burgh of Aberdeen; and this seems to be almost made certain from the fact mentioned by Mr. Gordon, that in his day the ruins of the old Tolbooth were to be seen close to the shore on the west side of the hill.

The Crofts of the Burgh form the next notable territorial division. They form a complete zone around the inhabited town. Their outer boundary is exactly known; and their inner boundary around the inhabited town is also distinguishable, and has been already described. These Crofts had in course of time each acquired a distinctive name and a fixed outline, so that before they were built upon any man acquainted with the town and its affairs could have pointed out the position and boundaries of each of them. Even now, although they have almost all been laid out in streets and covered with buildings, so that their original boundaries are obliterated, it is possible to distinguish them by examining the old title deeds of them and their various subdivisions. A little over thirty years ago it was found desirable to have them so traced out and identified, and the task was committed to Mr. John Stuart, now Dr. Stuart, and the late Mr. William Duncan, treasurer of police of Aberdeen. Both these gentlemen were well qualified for this work by their general antiquarian and special local knowledge. A blank map of Aberdeen was given to each of them, and working separately, and having access to abundant materials, they each produced a map of the Crofts completely filled up ; and on comparing the two maps thus separately constructed, the results were found to be practically identical. These maps are in the Town's charter room, and their publication would, I believe, be found exceedingly interesting.

The outer boundary of the Crofts, commonly known as the Town's Inner Marches, is described as follows in the later records of their periodical visitation and perambulation, viz., by a line commencing at the influx of the Ferryhill Burn into the river Dee, then holding up the said burn of Ferryhill to the east boundary of Damhead or Union Grove, turning up by the Justice Mill dam, and crossing the Skene turnpike road, leading from Union Place, and keeping along the east boundary of the lands of Rubislaw to the branch of the Skene turnpike road, which leads from Skene Street and the Schoolhill, thence crossing this branch of road and including Cherryvale, Hardweird, and the late Robert Mackie's property, to Jack's Brae, by a small lane, from thence turning towards the town by the road leading to Jack's Brae, and including the buildings from the house sometime occupied by William Reid on the north side of said road, and running along the north boundary of the ground connected with the said buildings till it reaches the enclosing wall of the property occupied by the Gilcomston Brewery Company, then keeping along that wall to a march stone at the gate leading to the Mill of Gilcomston, and passing through the kiln connected with that mill, and by a march stone till it reach the mill-lead or burn where there is another march stone, and along the back course of that burn by the Steps of Gilcomston, including the works used as a distillery by the Gilcomston Brewery Company, to a point opposite the gate leading to the Broadford Works, from this point, nearly in a straight line, to the point where the Burn of Broadford crosses the burn coming from Froghall and Causewayend, thence up the course of the last-mentioned burn to the Aberdeenshire Canal, at a point a few yards southwards of the canal lock, at or near Froghall, thence across the canal, and in a line to a march stone of the town of Aberdeen, marked No. 61, and from thence in a straight line to a march stone on the east side of the Spittal Road, near Love Lane, marked No. 62, thence eastward along the south boundary of the Spittal lands to the Old Town Links, and then turning northward by the east boundary of the Spittal lands, and along the Old Town Links till it joins the Tyle Burn, and keeping along the said burn to the river Don, then along the Don to the sea beach, and along the sea beach to the mouth of the Dee, then crossing it and keeping along the flood-mark on the south side of the river to the Craiglug, and there crossing the Dee and keeping the course of that river eastward to the point of commencement at the burn of Ferryhill.

In the old infeftments and other deeds contained in the records, pieces of ground lying within the old Burgh are described in some such manner as the following, " lying within the Burgh of Aberdeen," " at the east-end of Castle Street," " in the Netherkirkgate of the Burgh," " in Castle Street within the Burgh," " in Shiprow," &c. ; while lands lying among the crofts are generally described in such manner as, " in the east part of Aberdeen," " at the north end of the Burgh," " within the liberty of the Burgh," " in the territory of the crofts of the Burgh," " in the east territory of the crofts of the Burgh," &c., but occasionally they are described as " in the Burgh." As already noticed, Futty seems to have been a distinct townland, probably under the jurisdiction of the Burgh of Aberdeen, and to have been gradually incorporated with it. Lands lying in that quarter are variously described as " in the territory of the crofts of Futty " (1490), " in the burgh in Futty" (1503), " in Futty " (1503), " in the territory of Futty " (1528).

From these descriptions I think it is to be inferred that anciently the territory of the crofts was regarded as truly part of the Burgh, that the built and inhabited district had in common speech come to be generally mentioned as " the Burgh," and that the various styles of description quoted above had been adopted, not in any strict technical sense but only for convenience and distinctness.

The next great division of the Burghal Territories comprehended

the Forest of Stocket and the lands of Rubislaw and Cruives. Their
outlines were called the Outer Marches, and are thus described in the
records of their periodical perambulations. As these records are not
published, the length of the following description of a riding of the
marches two hundred years ago, with all its incidents, will be com-
pensated for by the interest attaching to it :—" 2nd August, 1673.—
The said day the provost, baillies, and certaine of the councell,
accompanied with certaine of the brethren of gild and deacons
of the craftsmen of airt, skillfull and expert in the tounis utter
marches, conform as they had been in use to be ridden yeirlie
past memorie of man, conform to the Acts of Parliament, the
burrows being convenit at the Womanhill, past, visite, red and
perambulat the utter marches and borders of the comon lands of
Aberdeen and freedom thereof, distinguishing the samen from out-
lands, lords lands, lyand and marchit contigue togither ; and first
bygane and took up their first march as the samen was wont to be
taken up of old at ane march stone at the south side of the Justice
Milne burne fornent the nuik of Collie's croft, contigue to the east side
of the king's gate, called the Hardgate, passand to the Bridge of
Dee at ane great stone, at the south side of the said gate markit with
ane sauser, which stone was fund to be in its right stance, and that
the new house latlie built be Ferrihill wis rightlie observit ; and not
upon the highway or within the march, and therefrae red in the said
gate upon the south syde of the house called the halfpennie house
and cornland at the back thereof on the west, north northwest of the
said house and gate to belong to the towne of Aberdeen as propertie
as many years before has been fund, and made interruptione by
taking of certaine diwats of the said houses, and cutting certaine of
the said cornes, and therefrae red on the said gate directly as march
of propertie to ane house possesseit by Magnus Keith, on the north-
west of the said gate forgainst ane little myre sicklyke upon the
tounis propertie and made interruptione as aforesaid : And therefrae
red in the said gate as march of propertie to ane place where ane
smiddie wes buildit and stood of old at the edge of ane strype wher
ther is ane march stone markit with ane sauser : And holding up
the way to certain housses situat and built together be Ferrihill and
his tennents, called Couperstoune, fund the said houses to be built
upon the touns propertie, and made interruptione throf as aforsaid :
As also of certaine corne land benorth and beweist the said housses
in manner forsaid ; and therefrae to ane stone beside Couperstoune

markit with ane sauser at the head of the myre in the hieway, and
bewest the samen betwixt the land of Pitmuckstone had incroatched
upon the loaning by making corne lande thereon, and made interruptione and appoynted ane stone with ane sauser thereon to be infixed
at the head of the rigg, going lineallie therefrae doune the dyke upon
the syde of the said corne lande : And frae the said march stone in
the myre holding up the strype to ane moss called Segiden, and fund
in the way certain holes made be morter leaders : And appoynted
them to be convenit and convict : And keeping the said gate souther-
lie or thereby to Collilaw to ane great craigstone markit with ane
sauser. Fund certain clods casten in the muir beyond Segiden be
the tennents of Ruthriestoune, and made interruptione and ordinit
them to be convenit : And from that Craigstone to ane great witter-
stone in the muir, markit with four holes wher ther is ane cairne set;
and from that to the fuird called Leslie's fuird, wher ther is ane stone
sett and markit with the toune of Aberdeen, their letter P. for propertie, wher ther is ane cairne upon the east syde of the fuird : And
remitting the marches betwixt the tounes commontie and the barronie
of Pitfoddels to the report of the visitors appoyntit for that
effect, past to the Cult gate keepand the said gate to the dame
of Pitfoddles, wher ther stood ane uther march stone of old,
markit with the syne of sauser haiving four witter holes : And ordainit the sauser therein to be deeper engraven : And ane sauser
to be made on ane stone upon the south syde of the burne a little be-
neth the dam : And frae the said milne dame to the black hill of
the Cults, where there is ane great march stone upon the brow of the
hill, haiving in it four witter holes : Ordainit ane sauser to be engraven therein : And therefrae direct south-wast to ane great witter
stone besydes Bells walls, haiving thrie holes on the syde and ane on
the top, and ordainit ane sauser to be made therein ; and therefrae
keepand the nether wall heids south west or thereby to the head of
the Den of Murthill, wher there is ane great sauser stone upon the
south syde of the muire at the head of the said Den : And finding
the marches betwixt Bells walls and the head of the Den of Murthill
not cleir, in respect some of the march stones had been tackin out,
ordainit for better clearing thereof in tyme coming ane stone lying
besouth Bells walls, a little above ane strype, and ane little rock
therein with ane pair of butts to the said stone to be markit with ane
sauser for ane marck in all time comeing as being in the direct way
according to the former perambulations to the said head of the den

of Murthill, and frae said march stone at the said head of the Den
of Murthill towards the weather Craig, and finding ane march stone
at the head of the said den of Murthill too farr distant from the
march stone at the weather Craig, appoynted ane great stone to be
markit with ane sauser, and infixed upon the top of ane round hillock
or know about midway betwixt the marches, upon which hillock
ane cairne is set : And from that to the Weddercraige where
there is ane stone markit with the syne of ane sauser : And from
the said Weddercraigge, northwest or thereby, to ane great
cairne on the Brunt hill markit with the syne of ane sauser :
And therefrae descending doune the said Brunt Hill north or
thereby to ane sink at the south side of the reisk and that part
of the said sink forgainst ane great craige on the south side
of the sink ; and fund that the laird of Culter, younger, or
others by his command, hade brunt and taken of ane sauser
of ane great stone march to the south side of the brae ; and
ordainit him to be legallie pursewit therefor ; as also he or his
tennents had casten peits upon the contravertit reisk ; made interruptione as aforesaid : and keepand the sink from the craige forsaid
while it enter in the burne callit the burne of Brotherfield, at that
part of the said burne wher ther is ane great gray stone standing on
ane hillock on the north side of the said burne, distant therefrae
ane halfe pair butts or therefrae descending doune the said burne
wastward, and keepand the midst of the reisk of the just and equal
half thereof to be on the south side of the said burne, which sall
belong to the lands of the lasts pertaining to Culter ; and the other
half of the said reisk to be on the north side of the said burne,
which sall belong to the lands of Brotherfield and Gairdaine of the
freedome of Aberdeen till it come to the fuird of the said burne,
under the hillock wher the houses stood of old biggit be James
Gordon, and sumtyme possesst be John Gordon of Crabstoune, then
called the Lasts, on the north syde of the which fuird the lands of Ord,
belonging before to the Earle of Marischall, and now to James
Raskine, and the lands of the freedome of Aberdene. And fund
that at the rottin the relict of Alexr. Forbes, in Brutherfield hade
made corne land of about ten pecks sowing, and ordainit her to be
convenit and convict thiranent, and inhibite to labor the same in
tyme comeing as being moss ground : And in respect the perambula-
tors of the said utter marches have been always heirtofoir necessitat
by reason of the unpassibleness of the way ouer the burne and

thorrow the maresh to keep the south side of the said burne and maresh, and to ryde and perambulat upon the lands belonging to the said laird of Culter, younger, which was not only much out of the ordinarie way, but also wes inconvenient for preservatione of their priviledges and libirties in that effair. Therefor fund it very expedient and comodious that ane calsie suld be built with all convenient diligence thorrow the maresh be east the Catcraig, to the effect the said visiters may have frie passage and ryde upon their awin bounds ; and that the dean of gild as thesaurier deburse the expenss thereanent which sall be allowit in their accompts, and Captain Dalgardnoe or any others the Councell sall appoynt oversee the cairfull makeing up of the said wark : And therefrae to the ringand stone by and on the west syde of the meadow of Bruther-field contigue to the brae of Ord, within the which meadow the relict of Master William Davidsone, and the said James Raskine now her husband, had sowine ane quantitie of bear and oats, whereof ane pairt cuttit and made interruptione, and frae the said brae of the Ord, keepand the saugh betwixt the meadow and the brae whill it come to the burne, fund that the relict of the said Alexr. Forbes of Brutherfield had made corne land of Bruntland, upon the moss at the muttons snell close to the bridge of the moss ; as also that Thomas Milne in Auchlie had made some corne land of moss ground near to the Bishop's dame ; as also that he had plougheit some moss ground upon the burne syde at the same place ; as also that the said relict had made corne land of moss ground, about six pecks sowing, upon the skirt of the moss of Brutherfield ; as also that the rind of the moss wes castin ; as also that Gilbert Mackie had laborit the end of four riggs of moss ground under Long Cairne, and ordainit the said Thomas Milne to be convenit and not to come further out upon the moss in time coming ; and that the said plougheit land ly unlaborit, and that the said relict labour not neir the moss by the length of ten oxin : And holding up and keeping the said burne to the fuird forgainst the houss of Brediauch, quhilk burne in certaine places the tenents of Kinmundie heid put out of its old track upon the lands of Kingswalls, and going up the said burne towards the rock wall of Kinmundie, ffand that the tenents of Kinmundie had castin great quantities of peits in the mosses of Borrowstoune, belong-ing to the toune of Aberdein, and made interruptione by cutting cer-taine of the peits, and ordenit the burne to be castin by ane streight lyne thorrow the midst of the moss to the rock wall, and from the

said rock wall till it come to the first march betwixt the toune and
the   at the inver of the said
burne, where the samen enters in the Black burne, which Black
burne devydes the lands of the Freedome from the lands of Easter
Kinmundie and Auchinleck, pertaining to the Earl of Marischall, at
that part of the said Black burne where ther is ane greit mortar
swell on the south syde of the said Black burne, direct forgainst and
anent the said inver, at which inver of the said Black burne ordined
ane stone to be unfixed for ane march, markit with ane sauser, and
set ane cairne thereat, and ascending and holding up the said Black
burne as the same goes north-eist thereby, ever keepand the sink and
the said Black burne at the south side of the hill called Eldrick
Hillock, whill it come to the heid of the Bluid burne wher there is
an little moss, and therefrae immediately thorrow the midst of the
said mosses, as the same is carneit (marked with cairns), whill it
enter in the Garlok burne, and descending doune the said Garlok
burne eist or thereby, as the samen runes betwixt two hills whill it
come to that part of chapman road where it crosses the said burne,
in which burne, at the pairt forsaid, there is ane cairne and ane
march stone markit with the seyne of ane sauser, and therefrae to ane
great march stone in the myre in the north syde of the hill of Brim-
mond, which was ordainit to be deeper engravin, at which stone there
wes ane cairne set, and therefrae holding and keepand the said chapman road whill it come to ane great march stone, markit with P. for
propertie, and finding that the possessors of the green well tree had
made corne land without the boundes, upon the tounis freedom, made
interruptione by cutting of the said cornes, and turneing in again to
the said hiegate ; and keepund the said chapman rod east or thereby
fund that Alexander Edward had made up certaine houses on the
freedome, and that beeist the said houses there wes certaine corne
land made be him on the freedome, and made interruptione, and
apoyntit Mr. James Sandilands of Craibstoune to be insistit against
for production of his evidents for cleiring the marches betwixt the
toune and him, as also for breaking ane sauser of ane march stone in
the way of the chapman rod, or some other to his knowledge ; and
keepand the said rod whill it come to the fuirde of the cross burne,
besouth the which rod the tenants of Cuparstone had castin
peits and sowin cornes within the mosses of Keplehill and made interruptione, and apoyntit march stones to be infixed on both sides
of the said chapman rod, markit with the signe of sauser, of com-

petent distance from uther, preserving ane hieway and rod all along
of fourteen foots of breadth, and croceand the burne and keepand
the march rode, stone be stone, as they are markit with the signe of
the sauser thorrow the cross of the Wagley whill it come to
ane stone markit with an sauser on the bank of the Bucks
burn, on the west syde thereof, abune the old dame and
fuird of the samen, and appoyntit ane stone to be fixed and
markit with ane sauser, at the fuird on the west syde of
the burne, as ane of the towns merches and that cairnes be set
about the merch stones on the chapman rod for better knowing
thereof, and frae the said sauser stone croceand the said burne, and
keepand the said dyck eastward to the auld dyke of Auchmull, whill
it come to ane march stone by and on the north syde of the gate and
keepand the said gate to ane march stone on the east syde of the
burne, within ane quarter of pair of butts or thereby thereto, and
holding therefrae, holding down the   burne, while it enter
the water of Done, and holding doune the water of Done whill it
come to the old found of the dira dyck, which dyck the tenents of
Hilltoune had broken doune and apoyntit the same to be made
up, and holding the said dyck southward while it come to the
craighead, where there is ane march stone markit with ane
sauser, and therefrae keepand the said dyck whill it come to
the teiled land of Caponstone, wher it was thought the old
kill of Caponstone stood, and there fund that the tenents of
Caponstone hid manured and taken in ane fauld of land upon the
touns freedome without the march, and made interruptione, and
holding down the laich eist or south-eist, or thereby, betwixt Collis-
touns dyke and the lands of Caponstoune to the fuird above Pick-
tillum, callit the Kings fuird, besouth which dyck it wes fund that
the tenents of Caponstoune hade taken in and made corne lande of
ane great piece of the freedome, and had riven out new ground to
ane considerable number of bolls sowing, which wes apoyntit to be
taken of to the tounes common good, besouth the march stone on the
hieway, which was found and ordenit to be markit with ane sauser
as the march in time coming, and made interruptione of the cornes
upon the said land, and therefrae keepand the said gate to ane
merch stone in the Den called Kettiebrauster, markit with ane sauser
and key, and therefrae keepand the north-eist gate, staine be staine,
as they are markit with sausers, thorrow the croft of Pictillum, in the
midst of which croft there is two merch stones markit with Saint

Peter's key, which in respect of the corne land could not be found, and appoyntit the said stones to be sought out and markit for merches in tyme coming, and therefrae, stone be stone, over the south end of the Spittell hill, as the same is markit with stones markit with the sauser and key, whill it come to the Gallowes Slackes, and ane eirdfust stone ther markit with the said sauser and key; and ordainit all comone loaning betwixt the land of Saint Peter's Hospital and the toune of Aberdeen which is found to be teiled and labored to be taken notice of, and ane loaning to be reservit, and merch stones accordinglie to be set; and therefrae doune the north side of the great snaill to ane strype called the Bansticle Burne, and fund that Mr. William Moirs tenents had built ane dycke alongst the land ends, and made interruptione; and therefrae keepand the said Bansticle Burne, as the same runs in the salt sea, and therefrae keepand the sea shore all along, under the blockhous and under the toune of Futtie and up the new shore, came to the Keyhead and upmost croune of the said burghe: Whereupon, and upon all and sundrie the premises, Alexr. Bennet, dean of gild, for himself, and in name of the Provest, Baillies, Councell, and communitie, asket and took instruments."

This line does not seem to include the river Dee beyond the Craiglug; but under the charters before-mentioned it is believed and held that the Burgh itself, the ancient Burgh, included the river and fishings as far as the Bridge of Dee; and it is evident that this is not mentioned in the perambulations, simply because the river itself was a well-known and reliable landmark which no encroaching neighbour could shift or remove.

When the Town some years ago feued out the last remaining lot of what was called the Commonty of Whitemyres, there remained of the unappropriated common land of the Burgh, only the Links. These lie within the territory of the Crofts as has been already shewn; but from the nature of their soil, they have always necessarily lain waste, and are now by use and wont prescriptively appropriated to the recreation of the inhabitants.

I have shewn that the Burgh lands, including the territory of the Crofts, the forest of Stocket, and the lands of Rubislaw and Cruives, are all held in burgage tenure of the Crown; and, therefore, we might expect that all the component parts of these lands should be held in burgage tenure of the Magistrates as the Baillies of the Crown; but it is not so. All the lands outside the inner marches are held in feu of the Burgh, and the authority for this has been explained. But a considerable part of the lands lying in the territory of the Crofts is found to be held in feu tenure without the Magistrates being acknowledged in the holding at all ; and this fact has given rise to a good deal of speculation and discussion amongst lawyers. Some have held it to be altogether an irregularity, and radically illegal. Others have supposed that it proves those feu lands not to have originally belonged to, or formed part of the Burgh. But the true explanation is to be found in the fact, that the feudal system of land tenure and its practical details did not spring at once into a complete and organised existence, and that at one time the distinction between feu and burgage tenure was not a real and important one, as it afterwards became. When the first charters to our Burgh were granted, there was no such thing in existence as a feudal tenure. The germ of the Burgage tenure then existed, but it was confined in its operation to the built and defended roods of the Burgh. These were held in free burgage—which meant simply that they were within the Burgh, that their holders were freemen, that they had the mercantile privileges of free burgesses, and that they were bound to fight for and defend the Burgh. At that time the word " feu" in our acceptation of it had no existence. The word " fee" is probably one of extreme antiquity, meaning simply treasure or value, and it was then used to express the right which that man had in any piece of land who paid scot or land tax for it, the " malar" or payer of mail as he was called, as distinguished from the right of its tenant or " few-fermar," that is of the man who farmed or rented the fee. It was also applied to lands held in burgage to express that the community, and none else, had right to the fee of the lands. Thus King Robert I., in his charter of 1320, gives to the burgesses of Aberdeen the Burgh and the Forest of Stocket, " ad feodifirmam," which at that date I take to have meant " for the purpose of farming out the fee of it," in terminable tacks or leases, and certainly not in feu-holdings as understood in more modern days ; and further the charter bears that it is to be held by them, " in feodo et hereditate et in libero burgagio ;" which means that the property was held in fee or feu, in the sense above explained, and also in free burgage. This mixing up of the terms since appropriated distinctively to feu and burgage tenure is quite common in old deeds, and proves that there was then no idea of their being contradictory or inconsistent. Thus in 1492,

David Wauss, vicar of Banff, gives a charter to John Chamer, of some crofts in Aberdeen, " to be held *from* me and my successors *of* our Sovereign Lord the King, in fee (feodo), and heritage and in free burgage . . . rendering thence annually, the said John, his heirs or assignees to our Sovereign Lord the King, burgage service for the said crofts used and wont as much as pertains to the same ; and paying to the said David Wauss " and to others, certain sums of money. And again in 1528, John Wauss, chaplain, gives to John Wauss, of Many, a charter of a croft in Aberdeen, " to be held *from* me, my heirs and assignees *of* the Lord of Saint John, preceptor of Torphiching, in fee and heritage, and in free burgage." Both these charters are recorded in the Burgh Register of Sasines of Aberdeen, and these are specimens of deeds, no doubt perfectly valid and regular in their construction, which exhibit lands held both in feu and burgage. To non-professional readers it may be well to explain that the character of these holdings as " feus" is not fixed, and does not depend upon the accuracy of my interpretation of the words " in fee" (feodo) but is certainly determined by the characteristic use of the words *from* and *of*.

The rest of the explanation is easy. In course of time the development of the practice of feudal conveyancing brought it about that it was held necessary that lands held in burgage-tenure should be held through the hands of the Magistrates as the King's Bailies, and not of the King directly, or of any subject superior. What then was to be done with lands held in both ways ? Probably some conveyances dropt out the feu, and held to the burgage-tenure ; but it is certain that many had dropt out the burgage and held to the feu-tenure. Next arose an idea that the Burgh Register should contain none but burgage-holdings, and the County Registers none but feu-holdings ; and when subsequently this was made imperative by an Act of Parliament, the distinction between the two manners of holding was changed into a reality, and there was no longer a choice between them. Those that were held in feu at that date must remain so ; and those that were then held burgage must remain burgage.

I am unwilling to declare my sketch finished while those remarkable words in the charter of King Alexander II., about " other burghs and burgesses within the bailiewick of Aberdeen" remain unexplained ; but as I cannot explain them, I have no choice. It may be noted, however, that at that period charters contained few superfluous words, and that whatever they did contain was put there for a purpose.

These are not words of style, nor are they there merely to fill up space. They are most unlikely words for such a purpose ; and they seem fully and distinctly to infer that, besides the settlement known as the Burgh of Aberdeen and its body of burgesses, there were, or recently had been, other settlements known as burghs, and other bodies of burgesses, within a district or jurisdiction known as the bailiewick of Aberdeen. It may be that Futty was one of these. It may be that the Burgh of Aberdeen, as then recognised, was com- · posed of a group of settlements which previously had been separate burghs, and were then only recently fused, or were in the process of fusion into one. But I am of opinion that if we could obtain a glimpse of things as they were—say when Columcille and Drostan came to Deer, we should find that a large space between Dee and Don was under the jurisdiction of a Bailie-Mor, whose seat was near the mouth of the Dee ; and that in course of time Gilcomston, Sea-town, Cruives, and Old Aberdeen had become detached from his jurisdiction. The two rivers near their mouths form so convenient and complete boundary lines that one can scarcely believe that the space enclosed between them had not formed one jurisdiction. But as the disjunction of portions of such a jurisdiction, say in the tenth or eleventh or twelfth centuries, would probably have been altogether in the King's discretion, and had involved no graver questions than giving some compensation or equivalent to the Magistrate whose ter-ritory was diminished, so the operation would leave little trace be-hind it. Only one recorded fact has come under my notice which seems to give evidence of the theory that the bailiewick had once comprehended Old Aberdeen, and it is a fact very circumstantially and distinctly related. In the Council Register of Aberdeen, under date 1st March, 1530, the following is recorded :—" The said day, William Lyon, balze to my lord of Abirdene, (*i. e.* The Bishop of Aberdeen), asket lycens at William Rolland, ane of the bailzeis of this burcht, to hang ane thief, quhilk was convickit in my lord of Aberdens Court, quhilk lycens the said William Rolland grantit, protestand that it sald nocht hurt the townis privilegis in na sort." Now the Bishops of Aberdeen from the time of the first Bishop Nectanus in 1134, were Barons in respect of their proprietorship of the " vill of Old Aberdon," besides a number of country parishes ; and in 1164 the Kirk of Saint Nicholas of Aberdeen was added to their Barony. Within the bounds of these possessions their baronial jurisdiction gave them right to try thieves and other criminals ; to doom them in certain cases to pit or gallows, and certainly to carry their sentences into execution.   In this case therefore it is a puzzle to say why the Bishop, if this thief was convicted in his own court, within his barony for a crime committed within his jurisdiction, should ask leave of the Bailies of Aberdeen to hang him ; and the only explanation that suggests itself is that the Bailies of Aberdeen being the King's Bailies, and therefore of higher judicial rank than the Bailie of a Baron, may have once had jurisdiction over the town of Old Aberdeen ; that this jurisdiction had never been expressly taken away, and that there had remained a traditional belief and claim that their criminal jurisdiction still extended over the whole of the ancient bailiewick.   This question of the extent of the ancient bailiewick of Aberdeen is interesting ; and, as I said before, much research might be necessary for its complete investigation.

We have now examined and beat the bounds of each of the three great divisions of the territories of the Burgh of Aberdeen—the Town, the Crofts, and the Forest—and although we have, as it were, seen the town outgrow its bounds, and overflow the field, and encroach on the forest ; although the distinctions between the three are now in fact practically blotted out and abolished, we see that they are clearly traceable, even as they were "'in days of yore, when Robert rang."   As to the nature of the right which a Burgess had in his rood of land within the town, we cannot see back to the time when no hereditary title was acknowledged, if such was ever the case ; but we see that even within our historical period the Burgess held his rood under conditions, viz., that it should be " biggyd and defendit," and by several enactments of the old Burgh Laws we find it declared that a man may sell land got by " conquest " (*i.e.*, purchase) freely, but that if it came to him by inheritance, he may not sell it without first offering it to the heir ; by which it would appear that the right of inheritance had been recognised and allowed earlier than the right of purchase.   As to the right allowed in the Crofts we have clearer knowledge.   Although they seem to have been the subjects of free sale and gift as far back as our land registers go, we nevertheless see that in theory such alienation was illegal, and that they were held to be, in theory, part of the inalienable common property of the Burgh.   Thus when, so late as the year 1559, the Magistrates meditated laying out some farther space for building about the higher part of the Schoolhill, they deemed it necessary to seek, and they obtained, a dispensation and license from the King to lay out building grounds, not for that particular locality only, but also for "onie pairt of the stretis, wayis, or common gaitis of our said Burgh of Aberdeen, or round about the samyn," and also a condonation and ratification of all former alienations, and a renunciation and discharge of "all actioun, criminall and civil, quhilk we or our farsaids may have againis theme for setting out of the pairtis before mentioned, or ony portion thairof." The Burgh with its Crofts was under a code of laws peculiar to Burghs, which constituted them military strongholds, and also the nurseries of commerce, and to some extent refuges for the oppressed. The nature of the right allowed to the occupiers of the Forest is still clearer. Until 1551 no part of the Forest was alienated from the community to private hands. It had been given by King Robert Bruce to the Burgh "*ad feodofirmam,*" and those who knew best what that expression was intended to mean interpreted it to the effect that only leases of moderate length were granted of its surface. In the last-mentioned year, however, Queen Mary, on a representation that strangers having no business or interest in the Burgh were in the habit of acquiring those leases, granted a licence to the Burgh to feu out these lands in perpetuity to Citizens and Burgesses, under certain restrictions which were afterwards removed. Till the Forest Laws gradually fell into desuetude, our Forest of Stocket had no doubt been governed according to those laws like the other numerous Royal forests in Scotland, whereof there seem to have been seven in Aberdeenshire, viz., Stocket, Dyce, Kintore, Benachie, Drum, Birse, and Braemar.

APPENDIX.

NOTE A.
KING DAVID'S CHARTER OF DATE 1134.

I find, too late for remarking upon it in the text, that grave doubts exist as to the authenticity of this Charter ; and yet even if these doubts are well-founded, they do not affect its value for the purposes for which it is here cited. Whether it be authentic or not, it was in existence, and is noticed by Boece, about the year 1400, and was believed by him to be genuine. This, therefore, carries its existence back to five hundred years ago, and probably a good deal further. The objection to it is that its form and the mode of its authentication were not in use in 1134 ; but there seems to be no improbability that in all its substantial elements it may be such a Charter as might have been granted by King David in 1134. It is not probable that an absolute forgery would have been executed and promulgated and received as authentic, between its alleged date and the days of Boece. The truth is supposed to be that the substance, and perhaps the very text, of the original Charter have been re-written, without any real or intended fraud or forgery ; and we must keep in view that at that early date much more respect was paid to the rights conveyed or confirmed by charters than to the documents themselves.

NOTE B.
NAME OF ABERDEEN.

By an authority too good to be slighted I am advised that the name of the Dee is not improbably derived from a Celtic word meaning black or dark, and the name of the Don from another Celtic word meaning green ; and that these distinctions had been suggested by the generally green aspect of the woods and haughs of Donside as compared with the brown heath-covered surface of the valley of the Dee.

NOTE C.
THE KIRK OF OLDMACHAR.

The ancient tradition that Saint Columba sent a missionary to the north-east coast of Scotland with instructions to look for a river whose windings near its mouth took the form of a crozier, or shepherd's crook, is generally regarded as incredible, because we assume that there is implied a miraculous or prophetic element in the saint's instruction ; whereas if we assume instead that the place had either been seen previously, or exactly described to him by some one who had seen it, the tradition ceases to be in any way improbable.

NOTE D.

MERCHANT GILD.

The Charter of King Alexander II. first specially recognises the existence and rights of a Merchant Gild. We have not, in modern history, any more curious fact than the existence and persistent continuance of this institution. No doubt the government of towns by an alderman and bailies was very ancient ; but the existence and authority of the Merchant Guild seem to have been at least equally ancient. These Guilds are said to have originated amongst the Scandinavian races, and to have had for their object the organisation and management of both warlike and mercantile enterprises. They are also said to have made a special point of nourishing sociality and abundant drinking. They naturally consisted of the most wealthy and influential members of the community, and therefore of those best fitted in these times to have the direction of local government. It was also a necessity of those times that the alderman, bailies, and Town Councils should be made up from the same class as the Guild. Any conflict between the two bodies would have been inconvenient, and ultimately destructive of the weaker. But both bodies were strong, and their interests were identical, and therefore they managed to agree, and divided the government between them. The Guildry was the body from which the civic dignitaries were usually chosen, but while the Alderman or Provost was the chief man of the community, the Dean of the Guildry held only the second place. The Dean of Guild came to be the officer at whose instance all the Burgh Laws were put in force, and all penalties and forfeitures sued for in the Burgh Court. Bailie Skene, in his Memorials tells us that he was the Procurator Fiscal of the Burgh. In course of time, however, he seems to have risen from the office of Procurator Fiscal, and to have assumed the office of a judge, while a paid official took the initiative in suits brought before the Burgh Court. Afterwards the functions of the Dean of Guild and those of the other magistrates came to be separated, the Dean confining himself to purely mercantile affairs and certain questions of boundaries and building ; the magistrates taking cognisance of other matters. The comparatively recent abolition of trading privileges took away a large portion of the Dean's work ; but at the same time his establishment in the second place in the Town Council left him in a position of honour and influence not inferior to that which he occupied when he first appears in history ; and however abhorrent his continued existence and exaltation may be to advanced liberalism, we find him vindicating his right to exist, and holding his enemies at bay, by the best of all defences, viz., usefulness and zeal for the public good.

The following is a copy of the Burgers' Oath, as used in the time of Queen Anne :—

Follows the B U R G E R S O A T H, to be sworn by all B U R-
G E S S E S of G I L D, and C R A F T S M E N of the Burgh of
A B E R D E E N the time of their Admission.

I Do solemnly Swear in the presence of *GOD*, that I presently own, profess and shall adhere to, and maintain the true Reformed *PROTESTANT RELIGION*, denying the Heresies of *Popery*, and *Quakerism;* and if I shall at any time hereafter (as *GOD* forbid) Apostatize from the said *PROTESTANT RELIGION*, by owning or professing *Popery* or *Quakerism*, I hereby Renounce all Benefite and Priviledge competent to Me as BURGES of ABERDEEN, alike as if I had never been admitted thereto.

I Do sincerely Promise and Swear that I will be Faithfull and bear true Alledgeance to Her Majesty Queen ANNE.

I Do solemnly Swear that I shall be obedient to the just and good Government of the said Burgh of ABERDEEN, and shall to the best of my power maintain and preserve the Peace and all the due Priviledges thereof, and particularly,

I.   I shall be leall and true to the said Burgh and Freedom.
II.   I shall never skaith their Wares.
III.   I shall foresee their profit, warn them of their skaith, and stop it to my power.
IV.   I shall obey the Magistrats and their Officers in all things Lawfull.
V.   I shall Vote no Person to be Provost, Baillie nor Counsellour of this Burgh, except Burgesses and actual indwellers within the same.
VI.   I shall give leall and true Counsell and advice, when it shall be asked.
VII.   I shall conceal the Counsell and Secrets of the said Burgh.
VIII. I shall own no Unfreemens Goods under Colour of mine.
IX.   I shall Scot, Lot, Watch, Wake and Ward with the Inhabitants of this Burgh.
X.   I shall purchase no Lordship Authority, nor Jurisdiction contrair to the Priviledges and Liberties of this Burgh, but shall maintain and defend the same to my Lifes End.

So Help Me GOD.

Addition for *CRAFTSMEN*.

I shall keep my self within the Bounds and Liberties of the Indentur past betwixt the Brethren of Gild and Craftsmen of this Burgh the *Seventh* of *July, One Thousand Five Hundred and Eighty Seven*. I shall be lyable to, and obey the *TOWNS* Statutes.

So Help Me GOD.

NOTA, That all *Chirurgeons, Apothecaries, Litsters, Barbers* and Others, who are not incorporat among the ordinar Trades, Do at their Admission as B U R G E R S, Swear the forsaid *Oath*, except the Fifth Article thereof, because they are only admitted BURGERS in *Sua Arte* allennarly, and are not BURGERS of Gild, nor Incorporat as said is.

NOTE E.
NAMES OF THE CROFTS.

Each croft had a name of its own, and the names seem to have arisen either from peculiarities of shape or size, as the Lyttel Croft, the Lang Riggs Croft, the Aucht Roods Croft, the Braid Croft, the Cruikit Croft; or from some building or other well known object of interest being on or near them, as the Angel Well Croft, the Dam Croft, the Ducot Croft, the Spittal Croft, the Cunninghairhills Croft, the Elfhill Croft, the Leper's House Croft, the Marywell Croft; or from some peculiarity of the soil or surface—as the Clayhills Croft, Fill-the-cup Croft, the Gutter Croft; or from some notable possessor of them as Barbour's or Edipingle's Croft, Collison's Croft, Coulli's Croft, Ymlay's Croft, Kynidei's Croft; while some of the names are not easily accounted for as Hardweird Croft, Sillieweird Croft, Sow Croft, Stancdeil Croft.

Sometimes the names of the crofts seem to have undergone change, as in the case of Barbour's or Edipingle's Croft. It is not certain which of these names is the older, but the latter was certainly named after its possessor, about 1360—Adam Pringle, a member of the Royal General Council, and of the Committee of Dooms, a burgess of Aberdeen, laird of the lands of Baudifash, in Aberdeenshire, Knoc in Strathauchin, Longforgund in Perthshire, and Whitsun in Berwickshire. The latter was his principal family estate; but at the period above mentioned it had been forfeited by the English conquerors, and Adam Pringle sojourned in Aberdeen until Scotland again got possession of the Border counties, when he was reinstated in the lands of Whitsun.

Adam Pringle's son Robert, built Smailholm Tower, in Berwickshire, about the year 1400. In 1388 he was armour-bearer or squire of the body to James, Earl of Douglas, at the battle of Otterburn, and held the same station about the person of Archibald, fourth Earl of Douglas (the Tyneman), and Duke of Turaine whom he accompanied, when sent to France with 10,000 auxiliaries to the assistance of Charles VII., and lost his life along with him at the battle of Verneuil, in 1424.

Such are the legends to which a study of the antiquities of a burgh like Aberdeen leads the way; and thus we learn the quality of our old Burgesses of Guild.

The Scottish tongue, prone to the use of diminutives, seems to have converted Adam into Adie or Edie, and the scribes of the north country, at that period probably semi-Celtic, preferred to write Pingle rather than Pringle. The identity of the man is certain.

NOTE F.
MIXED FEUDAL HOLDINGS WITHIN BURGHS.

The writer believes that he has met with instances of land within a Burgh being held, not as Burgage, but as part and parcel of Baronies situated " outwith " the Burgh; but he is unable here to specify any of them. That such had often been the case, however, seems to be proved by Article VI. of Fragmenta Collecta which is as follows :—" Item that the haill tenants of lands of a baronie within a burgh, aucht to be subject to the lawis of the burgh, and be corrected be the balyes anent brakand the asize price, and in all other causes and civil suits."

NOTE G.

THE RIVER DEE FROM THE CRAIGLUG TO THE BRIDGE OF DEE.

A confirmation of the idea that the ancient Burghal Jurisdiction comprehended this part of the river, has recently come to the writer's knowledge. The "Pott and Fuirds" salmon fishings, which occupy that part of the river, and which had from time to time within the last hundred years been asserted to be within the parish of Old Machar, and even the parish of Nigg, are found to be described in the older titles as lying within the Freedom of the Burgh of Aberdeen, Parish of Saint Nicholas, and Sheriffdom of Aberdeen.